HOW BRITAIN INITIATED BOTH WORLD WARS

Transcription of a talk given to the
London 9/11Keeptalking Group on
March 3rd. 2016

by Nick Kollerstrom, PhD

Contents

Europe in 1914

PART ONE –
WORLD WAR ONE

I LIGHT-HEARTEDLY GAVE this topic to Ian last summer, "How Britain initiated both world wars" and he's been going on since about me doing it, so I could not back out now ... We have done the idea of First World War initiation before[1], and will be recalling that.

This isn't about the history of the wars, it isn't about who are the good guys and who are the bad guys, it is the concept of initiating a world war - a very extraordinary concept - and who wanted it, who wanted it to happen. We do not accept that it just happened by itself, and I will try and argue that a will to war-initiation came from this country, and not some other country.

Let's start off in the months coming up to the First World War, May of 1914, when an American statesman reported back to America after a tour of Europe. He said, "The situation is extraordinary, jingoism run stark mad" - he was talking about the instability of the European nations - there was no way of avoiding this awful cataclysm, no-one in Europe can do it, it's locked into too many jealousies, and "… whenever England consents, France and Russia will close in on Germany and Austria."[2] [See slide 2, on page 27]

---

[1] See N.K., 'On the Avoidability of WW1' *Inconvenient History*, 2011,3, online.
[2] For this letter by US diplomat and presidential advisor Colonel E.House, concerning the pacific philosophy of the Kaiser, after a visit he paid in July 1914, see Buchanan, *The Unnecessary War*, p.22.

Now that is a very good summary of what happened, France and Russia would 'close in.' Let's have a look at the map here, how Austria-Hungary was about to be 'closed in' by Russia and France. [slide 3] Those were two nations which both wanted war -they believed they had territories they could only get back from Germany by war. The other nation that wanted war was Serbia, *but* not with Germany - it wanted war with Austria, because it had dreams of a greater Serbia, and it believed that war was a way of getting this, and it believed that, although it was smaller, Russia would support it.

So those were the countries that actually wanted war, and the situation was, that Russia would never have dared to go to war with Germany, unless it believed that France was supporting it, and France wouldn't have dared to support Russia in war against Germany, unless it believed that Britain was supporting it. Britain had as such no motive for going to war with Germany, unlike France or Russia. So the Question is, did Britain want to do it? Did it initiate this situation, this cataclysm?

It all depended on a French-English Entente which was secretive. This was woven from about 1905 onwards: a deal that if war broke out, France - which had been for centuries the traditional enemy of Britain - if war broke out, we would support France. Edward Grey secretly assured Poincarè that Britain would support France and Russia as an obligation of honour, if war broke out.[3] It was supposed to be a defensive alliance, but as this excellent book makes clear, *Hidden History, Secret Origins of the First World War* by Docherty &

---

[3] Grey was Britain's Foreign Secretary 1905-16 and Poincaré was the President of France 1913-20.

McGregor, it was really functioning as an offensive war-generating alliance [4]. This is the best book on the subject.

Bertrand Russell recalled how he was shocked by how happy people seemed to be, when war was declared, around the beginning of August[4]. Also, he always noticed how carefully Edward Grey concealed what he was doing [5] as he secretly committed us to war. The Government and the Cabinet and the people didn't realise this. We have here the concept of a secret elite: is it possible that a secret elite can drag this country into war?

Belgium was founded on a treaty of perpetual neutrality, which was supposed to guarantee that it would not take sides in a European war, but actually it had been making detailed war-plans with Britain in the event of war breaking out. Such things as stockpiles of cannon balls of the British standard not French, and coats for the soldiers, were found in Belgium, and when the Germans invaded Belgium they found agreements with Britain in the Belgian palace of government.[5] So Belgium was actually not neutral at all.

There was a deal for the hundred thousand British soldiers to be transported across to France and Belgium immediately when war broke out. Detailed plans had been made. So this meant that Germany realised that it was surrounded by not three but four hostile nations - it

---

[4] Bertrand Russell, *Autobiography,* Vol. 1, 1967, p.239.
[5] 'Britain and Belgium had been deeply involved in joint military preparations against Germany for at least eight years.' *Hidden History,* p.325.

was totally surrounded. This was the terrific deep fear and panic that built up and couldn't really be resolved.

Who was the Kaiser, Kaiser Wilhelm? He had quite a reputation as a peacemaker in Europe - here is the *New York Times'* judgment, made a year before, June 1913. [7] 'Now he is acclaimed everywhere as the greatest factor for peace that our time can show. It was he, again and again, who threw the weight of his personality into the balance for peace, whenever war-clouds gathered over Europe." That is quite fulsome praise. I would describe him as a wise peacemaker. Let's have another verdict, by a former US president, just before the war broke out: "…the critically important part which has been his among the nations, he has been for the last quarter of a century, the single greatest force in the practical maintenance of peace in the world." There was a BBC program, a centenary tribute to him which talked about his love of England and his deep attachment to Queen Victoria: the two Royal families shared the same ancestry with Queen Victoria.

In twenty-five years on the throne, he'd never gone to war and the German army hadn't fought a battle in nearly half a century. So it's reasonable to say that this was quite a pacific nation, whereas Britain and America had been to war quite a lot. He had a certain confidence in being able to use the strength of Germany to resolve issues of war and peace in Europe. If I may give you one more quote, from a very influential American statesman, Colonel House, he wrote a letter after visiting in July 1914, just before the war broke out. His letter to the Kaiser after his tour of Europe [10] recalled the wonderful conversations they had together: about how he the Kaiser had wanted to bring about a better understanding between the great powers: "because of your well-known desire to maintain peace, I came as your Majesty knows directly to Berlin. I can never forget the gracious acceptance of the general purposes of my mission, the masterly exposition of the world-wide political conditions as they exist today, and the prophetic forecast for the future." And he felt confident: "I live happy in the belief that your majesty's great influence was thrown on behalf of peace and the broadening of the world's commerce."

So we have had several judgments of the Kaiser, of him understanding how - if anyone could maintain peace in Europe - how it could be done. And then we get, just before the cataclysm, a friendly visit of the British Royal Navy to Germany. The new Dreadnoughts came to Kiel Harbour, and the Kaiser inspects a British ship wearing a British admiral uniform, to stress his connection with the British royal family.

So we wonder, how on earth could cataclysmic war break out, under these circumstances, between two nations that had been friendly for a thousand years? The assassination came at the end of June of the Austrian Arch-Duke, and it takes a while before anything happened then. All the Serbian newspapers were rejoicing at this assassination, so Austria has to respond.

The problem leading to both world wars, was that the geographical definition of Germany is smaller than the extent of the Germanic people. People who feel they are German, are wider than the boundary of what is fixed as Germany in 1871. For the first World War, that very much applies to Austria. The ruling family of Germany, since Mediaeval times had been in Austria - the

9

Habsburgs - and so there was a deep connection of Austria and Germany. Austria wanted to be part of Germany but wasn't allowed to: so this was in a sense what dragged Germany into the First World war.

Let's look at the development of the cataclysm, the sequence. Austria gives a severe ultimatum to Serbia, a ten-point ultimatum, what it's got to do - and, to everyone's surprise, Serbia nearly accepts them all, nine out of ten. But Austria is still angry, it was "'You've got to accept them all." The Kaiser insists: "This is capitulation, of the most humiliating sort, with it disappears every reason for war - every cause for war now falls to the ground". He tells Austria to accept that Serbian acquiescence. But he does not succeed in stopping - things happen too quickly now - he doesn't succeed in stopping Austria from shelling Belgrade in Serbia on 28th July.

One historian reckoned that they did it right away because they reckoned that, if they waited any longer, the Kaiser would have stopped them.[6] They were furious with Serbia and wanted to start shelling. The cataclysm begins, and the Kaiser angrily says, "Stop in Belgrade!" – that, this must not happen. He explains very clearly what has to happen now: this is the third time the Austrian army has been mobilized, so one has to do something - you can't just tell them to stand down. So he says, let the Austrian army go into Serbia and stand there

6 Harry Elmer Barnes, *The Genesis of the World War an Introduction to the Problem of War Guilt*, 1926, p.211 (2013 online): pressure from the Kaiser upon Austria for 'suspension of military activities and the opening of negotiations with Russia' as starting on 27th July.

and do nothing else. Just occupy part of Serbia, until the attempt to ascertain who did the assassination has been carried out satisfactorily, and then come back. No war - don't kill anybody, the army just goes in and stays there, it's a show of strength.

He says: "On this basis, I'm prepared to mediate for peace". [13] And I think you'll find that Grey said something rather similar. So, if there was time - *if* we had time - that would have been the peace formula. Which was what the Kaiser kind of assumed was going to happen, how to de-fuse it.

However, someone else on the scene had a different agenda. There's a long-predicted war agenda coming up, with Churchill in charge of the British navy, and the British navy has just been displayed to the King on the 26th of July. On his own initiative, he sends up - this is the largest fleet in the world - he sends it up to Scapa Flow north of Scotland, right outside Germany - and then, as the Kaiser said in his memoirs, he knew then that the war was coming. That's about the 28th of July: he knew that, once the British fleet is up there, that is the signal to all the warmongers in Europe - this is it, it's going to happen. The world's biggest navy cannot be sent up there without anything happening.

We note the psychology of Winston Churchill, the terrific happiness he felt as the war was approaching. All the other Cabinet members, the Liberals, they are all ashen-faced and despairing, with all the principles they have worked for all their life ... peace ... going out the window, as they are dragged into horrible war. Whereas Churchill was exultant, and he wrote to his wife Clementine, "My Darling, everything tends towards

11

catastrophe and collapse, but I am geared up and happy, is it not horrible to be built like that?" To someone else, a year later, he says, "Why, I would not be out of this glorious, delicious war for anything the world could give me." He gets a terrific thrill from managing it, moving the ships around and managing the war. [15] He loves war more than anything else, more even than brandy, or the sound of his own voice - he loves the war, and he gets on with it.

You'll find omitted, in a lot of WW1 books, the fact that the entire Royal Navy was sent up North, by Churchill's own initiative. How amazing is that? This is not the Prime Minister. This is the decisive war-initiating act. When we come to the Second World War, you'll find him as Prime Minister ringing up Bomber Command, on his own initiative, without having to tell anyone else. On his own initiative, he can send the fleet right up to its wartime base, in full battle-readiness. The whole of Europe was in a condition of fear, and there was the horrible argument that the war is going to happen anyway, so one might as well be first.

The Rothchilds have to come into this story somewhere, don't they? Nathaniel Rothschild visits Prime Minister Asquith to advise him of the preparations that the bank had put into place, to prepare for war.[17] This is late in July, and the meeting is 'to prepare for war,' to make sure that the Prime Minister has got the money and bank reserves available. There is the 'secret elite' - Grey, Asquith, Haldane and Churchill - these are people who are preparing for the coming war - they have said that it's going to happen, and how are they going to manage it? Parliament doesn't know a thing about this.

The great modern Revisionist, Henry Elmer Barnes, wrote in the 1950s - see the *Barnes Review* in memory of his work – he was a wonderful pioneer of modern Revisionism. What he called: "The moment when the horrors of war were specifically unchained in Europe" [18] - he puts on the 29th July, when Poincarè and Izvolski - these were the ministers of defence of France and Russia - met together, to finalise that they were going to war. The Czar of Russia doesn't quite know about this, he is very feeble, he keeps trying to tell the Kaiser that he isn't going to war, but he doesn't have the strength to resist it.

Hidden History says, the War was "deliberately and wilfully begun by Sazonov, Poincarè and Sir Edward Grey, at the bequest of the Secret Elite in London" [18] - I'm defending that thesis here, that they would not have had the nerve to do it without the Secret Elite in London telling them to do it. Here is a great Revisionist masterpiece, which should be on all your shelves really, by Patrick Buchanan, the wise American: *Churchill, Hitler and the Unnecessary War*, and this is the one mainstream book which Revisionists like and approve of. It's been a best-seller. Here is what he says: "By secretly committing Britain to war for France, these three - Grey, Churchill and Asquith - left the Kaiser in the dark, unaware that a war with France meant war with the British Empire." He had not been told that.

The German plan was to go quickly into France, beat France, and then fight Russia, because it couldn't fight the two of them together. That was the Schlieffen Plan. They weren't sure whether Britain would come in too - if Britain had said, yes we will come in too, then nothing would have happened - that would have stopped it from

13

happening. Thereby the European war was turned into a world War. There was a conflict going on in Eastern Europe, between Serbia and Austria, one backed by Russia and the other backed by Germany, and that was a local conflict, and the Kaiser was hoping to keep it local. But once the British fleet appeared on the Western coast of Germany, the Kaiser realized that this wasn't a local conflict, it was a conflict that didn't have any meaning other than Germany being done in. Britain had a choice here: there was as it were nothing impelling Britain to do this - I think that's very important.

On the 30th July, the Kaiser was still desperately telegramming the Czar, imploring him to stop mobilization. A million Russian troops had been mobilized, and there's a lot of debate, did mobilisation mean war? Well it makes it pretty damn likely. And he's begging him not to mobilize any more. "Serious preparations for war on my Eastern frontier. In my endeavours to maintain the peace of the world, I have gone to the utmost limit possible." [20] Germany was the last country to mobilise in Europe - if anyone tells you Germany started this war, the other countries all mobilised before Germany did.[7] "The responsibility for the disaster which now threatens the whole civilized world will not be laid at my door. In this moment it still lies in your power to avert it," he is saying to the Czar - which is technically quite true. "My friendship for you and your empire, transmitted to me by my Grandfather on his deathbed, has always been sacred to me, and I have always honestly backed up Russia when she was in serious trouble." So he's reminding how he'd helped

---

[7] *Hidden History*: "Germany was the last of the continental powers to take that irrevocable step [of mobilization]" p.321.

Russia in the past. "The peace of Europe may still be maintained by you" - if he [the Czar] could stop the military build-up. He's still believing that he can maintain the peace of Europe. This is right at the end of July.

The timetable of the disaster [21] shows how Russia is mobilising right at the end of July: the Kaiser sends his telegram to the Czar, and around the end of July we get the irrevocable French decision to support Russia, that is shown in [French] telegrams, which can be documented. France was kind of pretending, it kept its troops ten miles from the border, it was trying to tell Britain that it wasn't going to war, that it wasn't committed, but I think documents show that it was.

On the first of August we get a vital conversation of the German ambassador Lichnovsky with Grey in London. This is as it were the last attempt by the Kaiser to get a peace deal with Britain.

All the Cabinet except Grey and Churchill are in favour of total neutrality, that if war breaks out Britain does not come in. In a way, you could say that the war came because Britain didn't make its position clear: if it had clearly said, No we're not coming into the war, then France and Russia would not have gone into it. So it was the ambivalence of Britain which kind of led to this disaster.

Right at the end of July Kaiser Wilhelm writes in despair in his diary - he realises he's trapped, he realises he cannot stop the war, there's nothing he can do: "The most frightful war, of which the ultimate aim is the overthrow of Germany" - so it's not a question of maintaining peace between Serbia and Austria, it's a war against Germany. because people want to *do in* Germany. In a way, it hasn't got a rational purpose, that's the terrible thing, that's why diplomats couldn't resolve it. "I no longer have any doubt, that England, Russia and France have agreed amongst themselves, knowing that our treaty obligations compel us to support Austria, to use the Austria-Serb conflict as a pretext for waging a war of annihilation against us." He alludes to, "A purely anti-German policy which England has been scornfully pursuing" - Germany can't escape from it. [22]

Grey is very duplicitous - he's an honest-sounding fellow, and he had a terrific reputation as Britain's Foreign Secretary, but he had this duplicitous role. Here's the writer H.G. Wells making his final judgment: "I think Grey wanted the war, and I think he wanted it to come when it did." The great paradox is, that everyone in Europe after the war said, We didn't want it, no, we did our best to avoid it. So you've got, nine million people die, then everybody in Europe says they didn't want it - afterwards. "The charge is, that he did not definitely warn Germany, that we would certainly come into the war. He was sufficiently ambiguous, to let them take the risk, and he did this deliberately." That is a final judgment of H.G.Wells, which I think is pretty sound.

August 1st, people begin to realise, suddenly, of some disaster impending, that someone's going to pull us into this war, of which we've had no notice. The *Daily News* says, "The greatest calamity in our history is upon us. At this moment our fate is being sealed by hands we know not, by motives alien to our interests, and by influences which, if we knew, we would certainly repudiate." [24] How true! That sums up the way in which hidden forces

16

made the deal, that pulled Britain into war.

There is a very good author, Morel, *Truth and the War*, and he referred to "Those dreadful fields of senseless carnage" as the soldiers were fighting each other on the fields of Flanders. We were fighting a country which had never ever threatened us in our entire history, and the flower of British youth was dying there. And what the hell was it for? As Morel so clearly said of the alliance with France: "While negative assurances had been given to the House of Commons, positive assurances diametrically opposed had been concocted by the War Office and the Admiralty. All the obligations of an alliance had been incurred by dangerous and subtle methods, in such a way as to leave the Cabinet free to deny its existence." Here is Albion speaking with a double tongue! It's a two-forked language, whereby Parliament was constantly being told, we have no obligation for war - no of course not - but actually, detailed war-plans have been made, all ready to be activated – which very soon happened.

Another good book is *How the War Came* by Lord Loreburn (1919). Let me say, there is virtually no modern book on this subject which I recommend, except for the *Hidden History* which has come out recently. These are old, Revisionist classics which I'm recommending here, which manage to, I think, get the ambiguity of what really happened. "Edward Gray slipped into a new policy, but without either Army, or treaty, or warrant of parliamentary approval. This country has a right to know its own obligations, and when the most momentous decision of our whole history had to be taken, we were not free to decide… A war to which were committed beforehand in the dark..." [26]

17

Parliament was only told on the 3rd!

Parliament first heard about the coming war, by means of a stirring speech by Edward Grey on August 3rd and then - no questions, no discussion! No discussion! Does it remind you of the Iraq war, or what? Parliament is suddenly given this emotionally traumatic announcement: because of an invasion of Belgium that *has not yet happened*, that is due to happen, we've got to go, we have to start a war, quickly! After giving his masterly talk, Grey then walks out - No sorry, we can't discuss the matter. And that was the way of informing the country and parliament, by that speech. So, as Lord Loreburn says here, "Parliament found itself at two hours' notice, unable, had it so desired, to extricate itself from this fearful predicament."[8]

Belgium was invaded the next day on the 4th, so the talk was *in anticipation of* this event.

I came to this story in my youth, reading the Austrian philosopher Rudolf Steiner, who had been giving talks in December, 1916. So I heard the German point of view, it was the only time I'd ever heard a German point of view concerning the War. And that was terribly moving, because December 1916 was when Germany had offered a peace deal to Britain, which was being declined. Germany said, Look, whatever the point of this war is, can we just stop? Can we just go home, and be friends again? It's called *Status quo ante* - and even the American government encouraged this, they said, It's a good peace deal, why doesn't Europe stop fighting? But no, we had to go on, because .. well, why? Let's not go

---

[8] Loreburn, 1919, pp.16.

into why, I'm sure we all have our own views, as to why Britain could not accept the peace deal.

I remind you that we are only concerned with the initiation of war - who *wanted* to start the war? That's all we are looking at today. Steiner made the very outrageous statement, that "With a single sentence, this war in the West would not have taken place:" that, if Grey had given a straight answer to Lichnovsky, then we could have avoided the catastrophe that took place. Here is the event which is missed out from just about every book on WW1. Any book you've got on your shelf, have a look at it and it won't have this event, on the first of August – *but* it cannot be written out of history, because Grey sent off a letter that same afternoon, saying exactly what you read here - and it went into the British White Book, the record of war documents.[9] It's in there, you can read it.

No one can deny that Grey summarized the meeting in this way: "Lichnovski asked me whether, if Germany gave a promise not to violate Belgian neutrality, we would engage to remain neutral." Huh, what more do you want? "I replied that we could not say that, our hands must be free." No commitment - even though the British fleet has gone up North - no commitment! So, "We could not give a promise on that condition alone". That is an amazing, staggering offer that Lichnovsky makes, to avoid war with Britain. And, he then asks a further question: "he then pressed me on what conditions, on which we would remain neutral" - any conditions, on which Britain would remain neutral. "He

---

[9] *British documents on the origins of the war 1898-1914,* Vol XI, HMSO 1926.

even suggested the integrity of France and her colonies might be guaranteed." Well, what more do you want? Not only did Grey refuse to reply, but - get this - he didn't mention this interview to Parliament. When he gave his speech he made no mention of the fact that this interview with the German ambassador had taken place just before. And he tried to pretend that he thought it was just a personal meeting.

This was the final attempt by the Kaiser, and there is a story that he heard the news back from Lichnovsky, and he misunderstood it. He thought there was a deal made - this is late afternoon of the 1st of August - he said, let's open a bottle of champagne, or something, there's some hope. And he thought there was some sort of agreement. And he told von Moltke, head of his military - Stop! The troops were already going towards the Belgian border, and he said, stop them! And von Moltke said, We can't do that, that is impossible. Von Moltke was totally traumatized that day. Then later the King of England contacted the Kaiser and told him, no there had been no agreement, it was a misunderstanding.[10] And that was as it were the end of the Kaiser's role in the war, and basically the end of the German royal family, it was the last royal dynasty. He didn't really play any further role in the war once his final struggle to avoid war had been defeated and outwitted. He'd been outwitted by the British, by this clever *double entendre* of, will we / won't we.

Various people on the Continent have discussed and evaluated that meeting - not in Britain of course, you won't find any historians discussing that meeting on

---

[10] *Hidden History*, p.321.

August 1st in any British college, it just gets deleted from the books, except for this one recently[11], this is the only one that has it. "Prince Lichnovsky asked if Britain would agree to remain neutral if Germany refrained from violating Belgian neutrality. Sir Edward Grey refused. Would he agree if Germany was to guarantee the integrity of both France and her colonies? No." [29] Now, that is a fair summary of what Germany asked, as a way of avoiding the war. So if there had been a will to avoid the war, can we agree that that is the last possible date on which an answer could have been given that could have avoided the war? Nine million people need not have died, if Grey had given a straight answer: 'Yes that sounds like a great deal, let's shake on it.' That was the last possible moment on which the catastrophe could have been avoided, which extinguished all the bright hopes and optimism of European civilization.

Here is a nice simple summary of the enigma, which a US President gave, years later, when the war was all over: "We know for a certainty that, if Germany had thought for a moment that Great Britain would go in with France and Russia, she would never have undertaken the enterprise." [30] Now you should all appreciate, the enterprise here was the Schlieffen Plan - that if you are threatened by attack from Russia, which Germany was, you go into France, beat France, and then you can take on Russia - which sounds sort of horrific now, but that was the plan. It was a defensive plan, the only one they had. So, going into Belgium was Germany's defensive war-plan.

This is what one might call an early conspiracy-theory

---

[11] Ibid, p.322.

view, of what caused the war, that the people visible in Britain, namely Churchill and Grey and Asquith, who were making the war happen, were puppets., and behind them was an influential group. Rudolf Steiner said that this war was not wanted by people in Germany, there was not a force for war in Germany, that would be unthinkable.[12] Germany wanted cultural growth and trade. He said: "Behind those who were in a way the puppets, there stood in England a powerful and influential group of people, who pushed matters doggedly towards a war with Germany, and through whom the way was paved for the World War that had always been prophesied. How powerful was the group, who like an outpost of mighty impulses stood before the puppets in the foreground. These latter are perfectly honest people, yet they are puppets, and now they will vanish into obscurity." He is saying that people, who we might nowadays call the international bankers, or the Illuminati or freemasons or whatever, were behind these public figures.

> Reply to floor comment: The Kaiser desperately wanted a friendship deal with Britain, where Germany was the main land-power and Britain rules the waves: couldn't there be some peace deal between them? He was very baffled that it couldn't be, and it couldn't be because of what we may call the Churchillian doctrine, that Britain always had to oppose the strongest power in Europe: an everlasting-war policy. That was the grounds on which Britain said, no we can't have a deal of security and peace with Germany. So tragically that couldn't happen.

---

[12] Steiner, *Karma*, pp.84-5

We're on the 3rd of August now, and this is the day when Grey makes his speech to the Commons, on the grounds of Germany going into Belgium. Germany had politely asked Belgium if it could go through into France - a gentleman here [in the audience] says it was an invasion of Belgium, but there were legal precedents, of Britain asking permission to go through a country, to go to war - on being asked that, Belgium immediately contacted the British government to say it had been asked by Germany if it could go through, and it was all-important for Britain that Belgium said, No, you cannot go through, as that was going to be the grounds on which Britain could declare war. Here is what Bernard Shaw said: "The violation of Belgian neutrality by the Germans was the mainstay of our righteousness. I guessed that, when the German account of our dealings with Belgium reached the United States, it would be found that our own account of the neutrality of Belgium was as little compatible with neutrality as the German invasion[13]."[33]

We did not have a very righteous position in alluding to the [Belgian] Treaty of Perpetual Neutrality, because as mentioned Britain had already violated it. Britain's Prime Minister Asquith made a speech explaining why Britain had entered the war (on August 6th) based on the lie that that that treaty obliged us to come to the rescue of Belgium. That Treaty had no clause whatever obliging countries to come to the defence of Belgium if it was invaded.

If I may quote again from *Hidden History*: "Germany

---

[13] Ross, p.42.

offered Belgium friendly neutrality, if a safe passage

35 US poster, **The Phantom Menace**

could be allowed, because in its defence against France it had to have passage across Belgium." [34] There were precedents: in the Boer war British troops were permitted passage across neutral Portuguese territory, to fight in South Africa, so this was regarded as having a legal precedent. It isn't just an invasion - though in a sense, because Belgium said no, there was fighting.

What we may call the 'Phantom Menace' appears here as a horrific image of Germany, as if it were liable to come up onto the shores of America – atrocity propaganda for America, "Destroy this mad brute!" Massive lies were created by Britain's Ministry of Information, and it was found after the war that none of it had been true.

> Audience Comment: They shredded the archives of the lie-factory at the end of the war.

This is a book which I recommend, *Propaganda for War*, it's very much from an American point of view. It's an excellent book about the atrocity propaganda from the first World War. (An earlier book, is the old classic *Unconditional Hatred* by Captain Grenfell.) I'll just quote from it: "As passions cooled after the war, the gigantic lies created by American and British propaganda, were one by one exposed to the light." There is only one authenticated atrocity story from the First World War, and that was the illegal blockade of Germany, which extended till after the war, so that about seven hundred thousand people died of starvation, that was the one authenticated atrocity of the First World War. Furthermore -you don't have to agree with me here

- I would say that there was an asymmetry here, whereby the atrocity propaganda was mainly on the British and American and somewhat French side, but not on the German side. The Germans didn't have the same concept of fabricating untruths to motivate their troops.

> Audience comment: A week before, on July 25th, the British treasury began printing special notes that were marked 'for war expenses.'[14]

Many believed that a mistake made by Germany leading to the war, was its building up a navy to rival Britain's, which led to an arms race, a huge military arms race. Germany said, we've got colonies, so we have to have a navy - some people said that was the great disaster, that they should not have done it. So here's a view from 1925, if you'll excuse me quoting Adolf Hitler, looking at what he thought was the terrible mistake which needed to be avoided. He was wondering, how friendship with Britain could be achieved, and why had it failed so badly in the war? "No sacrifice should have been too great … We should have renounced colonies and sea-power, spared British industry our competition." [37] Germany should remain a land power. Renunciation of a German war-fleet and power of the land army - that would, he reckoned, be the key to not aggravating

---

[14] 'The Bankers secretly devised a scheme by which their obligations could be met by fiat money (so-called treasury notes)' to pay for the war: 'The decision to use treasury notes to fulfil the bankers' liabilities was made as early as July 25 The first treasury notes were run off the presses …on the following Tuesday July 28th, at a time when most politicians believed that Britain would stay out of the war.' Carroll Quigley in *Tragedy and Hope, a History of the World in Our Time,* 1966, p.317 (Thanks to J.W. for this reference).

Britain, whereby they could have peaceful, friendly relations in the future.

Finally, here is a review of a hundred years of friendship and enmity of Germany and England - *Best of Enemies*, by Richard Milton. He referred to Britain's propaganda machine as "An infernal engine created in war but impossible to switch off in peace." We may reflect upon the main thing to have come out from the First World War, in his view:

> The indelible memory of atrocity stories that had taken place only in the imaginations of British propaganda agents proved to be stronger and more persistent than any facts.

* * * * * * *

SLIDES USED

Image: Your Country Needs You

2 Report by Col. Mandell House, May 1914:
The situation is extraordinary. It is jingoism run stark mad. Unless someone acting for you [Wilson] can bring about a different understanding, there is coming some day an awful cataclysm. No one in Europe can do it. There is too much hatred, too many jealousies. **Whenever England consents, France and Russia will close in on Germany and Austria.'**

4 French position:
Under Poincaré, the nature of the Franco-Russian alliance was fundamentally committed to war, not defence. Thus he visited Sazonov in St Petersburg to reassure him of French and British commitment to war with Germany... Edward Grey secretly assured Poincaré that Britain would support France and Russia as 'an obligation of honour' should the Balkan trouble lead to a European war.' - Docherty & McGregor, *Hidden History*, 2013, p.209, 236

5 Bertrand Russell's Autobiography
'I had noticed during previous years how carefully Sir Edward Grey lied in order to prevent the public from knowing the methods by which he was committing us to

the support of France in the event of war.'

6. Belgian non-neutrality:
According to evidence later published in New York, the
Belgians were advised in November 1912 by the British
military that as soon as a European war broke out,
160,000 men would be transported to Belgium and
northern France, with or without the permission of the
Belgian government   - *Hidden History*, p.237

7. Kaiser as peacemaker
'Now ... he is acclaimed everywhere as the greatest
factor for peace that our time can show. It was he, we
hear, who again and again threw the weight of his
dominating personality, backed by the greatest military
organisation in the world – an organisation built up by
himself – into the balance for peace wherever war clouds
gathered over Europe.'
        - *New York Times*, 'William II, King of Prussia
and German Emperor, Kaiser 25 years a ruler, hailed as
chief peacemaker', 8 June 1913

8. Kaiser as peacemaker – 2
   A former US President, William Howard Taft, said of
him: 'The truth of history requires the verdict that,
considering **the critically important part which has
been his among the nations, he has been, for the last
quarter of a century, the single greatest force in the
practical maintenance of peace in the world**.'
        In 1960 a BBC centenary tribute to the Kaiser was
permitted to say: 'Emphasis was placed on his love of
England and his deep attachment to Queen Victoria,' his

grandmother.

Never had the Kaiser gone to war in 25 years on the throne, nor had the German army fought a battle in nearly half a century.

9   Kaiser Wilhelm

10 Colonel House's view of the Kaiser, 8 July 1914

Sir!

Your Imperial Majesty will doubtless recall our conversation at Potsdam, and that with the President's consent and approval I came to Europe for the purpose of ascertaining whether or not it was possible to bring about a better understanding between the Great Powers … Because of the commanding position your Majesty occupies, and **because of your well-known desire to**

maintain peace, I came, as your Majesty knows, directly to Berlin. I can never forget the gracious acceptance of the general purposes of my mission**, the masterly exposition of the world-wide political conditions as they exist today and the prophetic forecast as to the future which your Majesty then made.** I received every reasonable assurance of your Majesty's cordial approval of the President's purpose, **and I left Germany happy in the belief that your Majesty's great influence would be thrown in behalf of peace and the broadening of the world's commerce**...

Edward House

11 Friendship Fest

June 23, 1914: Royal Navy battle squadron with new dreadnoughts sails into Kiel harbour. The Kaiser, wearing British admiral uniform, inspects the *King George V*.

June 28: assassination of Archduke Ferdinand.

12 Austria's Ultimatum

24 July: Austria gives ultimatum to Serbia

26 July: Serbia accepts 9 out of 10 of Austrian demands.

The Kaiser: 'It was capitulation of the most humilating sort. With it disappears every reason for war ... Every cause for war now falls to the ground.'

27th   Austria declares war.

28th   Belgrade is shelled.

The Kaiser writes: 'Stop in Belgrade!'

13 The Kaiser's Advice

31

14 Churchill: the First Sea-Lord

The Kaiser advocated a temporary military occupation: *Let the Austrians occupy Belgrade until Serbia accepts their demands – but stop at that.*
'On this basis, I am prepared to mediate for peace.' - *Hidden History*, p.290

15 A Happy Man

'Churchill was the only minister to feel any sense of exultation at the course of events' (his biographer John Charmley, on the days leading up to the War)

Churchill to his wife Clementine: 'My darling one & beautiful. Everything tends towards catastrophe and collapse. I am interested, geared up and happy. Is it not horrible to be built like that?'

'Why I would not be out of this glorious delicious war for anything the world could give me.' (Margot Asquith's diary, January 1915)

16 Churchill sends British fleet to Germany on 28 July

On July 26th, a 'Test Mobilisation' of the entire Royal Navy paraded before the King at Spithead, after which the Navy was held in full battle-readiness.
'Churchill, upon his own responsibility and against the express decision of the Cabinet, ordered the mobilisation of the Naval Reserve.' On the 27th, 'the fleet [was] sent North'   - Hugh Martin, *Battle, the Life-story of the Rt Hon. Winston Churchill,* 1937. Churchill secretly ordered the core of the fleet to move north to its protected wartime base .. riding at top speed and with its lights out, it tore through the night up the North sea.'   - Adam Hochschild, *To End All Wars,* 2011, p.85.

17 To Prepare for War

Lord Nathaniel Rothschild made an unscheduled visit to Prime Minister Asquith to advise him on the preparations that his bank had put in place **to prepare for war** (Late July, 1914) - *Hidden History,* p.290.

The Secret Elite meet:
29th July: Grey, Asquith, Haldane and
Churchill had a meeting to discuss what
Asquith called 'the coming war.'

18 Harry Elmer Barnes, on war-initiation
 The secret conference of Poincaré, Viviani and
Messimy, in consultation with Izvolski, on the night of
29th of July, marks the moment when the horrors of war
were specifically unchained in Europe. - Barnes, *The
Genesis of the World War 1926 p.242*
Compare:
War was 'deliberately, wilfully begun by Sazonov,
Poincare and Sir Edward Grey, all at the behest of the
secret elite in London.'   - *Hidden History,* p.297

19 The Secret Deal
    By secretly committing Britain to war for France,
Grey, Churchill and Asquith left the Kaiser in the dark,
unaware that a war with France meant war with the
British empire.
    Britain turned the European war of August 1 into a
world war...
    For Britain, World War 1 was not a war of necessity
but a war of choice.' -*Buchanan, The Unnecessary War*
pp.50, 64

20 Kaiser telegrams Czar, 30 July
 I now receive authentic news of serious preparations
for war on my Eastern frontier. ... In my endeavours to
maintain the peace of the world I have gone to the
utmost limit possible. The responsibility for the disaster

which is now threatening the whole civilized world will not be laid at my door. In this moment it still lies in your power to avert it… My friendship for you and your empire, transmitted to me by my grandfather on his deathbed has always been sacred to me and I have honestly often backed up Russia when she was in serious trouble especially in her last war.

The peace of Europe may still be maintained by you, if Russia will agree to stop the military measures which must threaten Germany and Austro-Hungary.

21 Timeline of war-outbreak

26th July: King reviews British fleet at Spithead, Churchill instructs it not to disperse.

27th   Grey tells parliament he will resign, if Cabinet does not support his go-to-war-for-France policy. Churchill orders British fleet up to Scapa Flow.

29th   Russia mobilised

30th   Kaiser telegrams Tzar, 'The peace of Europe may still be maintained…'

31st   Evening: French government 'irrevocably decides' to support Russia.   French troops enter Belgium

1st August, 1 am: French Govt. cables Russia, its war-support   Noon: Grey – Lichnowsky conversation in London   Night: Germany declares war on Russia and mobilises

1st-2nd All Cabinet except Grey & Churchill are pro-British neutrality.

2nd   Grey gives France the assurance of war-support. French planes flying over Belgium,   German govt. warning to Belgium over neutrality violation

Tuesday 4th   Germany invades Belgium, UK declares war on Germany, and then cuts the trans-Atlantic telephone cables from Germany

22 Kaiser Wilhelm's diary 30-31st of July

Frivolity and weakness are going to plunge the world **into the most frightful war of which the ultimate object is the overthrow of Germany. For I no longer have any doubt that England, Russia and France have agreed among themselves – knowing that our treaty obligations compel us to support Austria – to use the Austro-Serb conflict as a pretext for waging a war of annihilation against us...** In this way the stupidity and clumsiness of our ally [Austria] is turned into a noose. So the celebrated encirclement of Germany has finally become an accepted fact... The net has suddenly been closed over our heads, and **the purely anti-German policy which England has been scornfully pursuing all over the world has won the most spectacular victory which we have proved ourselves powerless to prevent while they, having got us despite our struggles all alone into the net through our loyalty to Austria, proceed to throttle our political and economic existence.** A magnificent achievement, which even those for whom it means disaster are bound to admire.

23 H.G.Wells on Grey's role

'I think he (Gray) wanted the war and I think he wanted it to come when it did ... The charge is, that he did not definitely warn Germany, that we should certainly come into the war, that he was sufficiently ambiguous to let her take a risk and attack, and that he did this deliberately. I think that this charge is sound. Autobiography

24 *Daily News*, August 1

'The greatest calamity in history is upon us ... At this moment our fate is being sealed by hands that we know not, by motives alien to our interests, by influences that if we knew we should certainly repudiate

25 "Those dreadful fields of senseless carnage"

'It came therefore to this. While negative assurances had been given to the House of Commons, positive acts diametrically opposed to these assurances had been concerted by the War Office and the Admiralty with the authority of the Foreign Office. All the obligations of an alliance had been incurred, but incurred by the most dangerous and subtle methods; incurred in such a way as to leave the Cabinet free to deny the existence of any formal parchment recording them, and free to represent its policy at home and abroad as one of contractual detachment from the rival Continental groups.   - E.D. Morel, *Truth and the War,* 1916

26 The Secret Deal with France

'The final mistake was that when, on the actual crisis arising, a decision one way or the other might and, so far as can be judged, would have averted the Continental war altogether ... The mischief is that Sir Edward Grey slipped into a new policy, but without either Army, or treaty, or warrant of Parliamentary approval ... This country has a right to know its own obligations and prepare to meet them and to decide its own destinies. When the most momentous decision of our whole history had to be taken we were not free to decide. We entered a war to which we had been committed beforehand in the dark, and Parliament found itself at two hours' notice unable, had it desired, to extricate us from this fearful predicament... - The Earl Lorenburn, *How the War Came*, 1919

27 'With a single sentence'

'A single sentence and the war in the West would not have taken place... It is really true that Sir Edward Grey could have prevented it with a single sentence... History will one day show that the neutrality of Belgium would never have been violated if Sir Edward Grey had made the declaration which it would have been quite easy for him to make.' Rudolf Steiner in December, 1916, concerning the meeting on August 1, 1914: *The Karma of Untruthfulness*

28 Grey, on his meeting with Lichnowsky, 1 August

'He asked me whether, if Germany gave a promise not to violate Belgian neutrality we would engage to remain neutral. I replied that I could not say that: our hands were still free, and we were considering what our attitude should be....I did not think that we could give a promise on that condition alone.
The ambassador pressed me as to whether I could formulate conditions on which we would remain neutral. He even suggested that the integrity of France and her colonies might be guaranteed. I said that I felt obliged to refuse definitely any promise to remain neutral on similar terms, and I could only say that we must keep our hands free.' - Britain's 'Blue Book,' HMSO, 1926, p.261.

29 A Summary of the August 1 meeting

'Now Prince Lichnowsky, the German Ambassador in London, asked whether England would agree to remain neutral if Germany refrained from violating Belgium's neutrality. Sir Edward Grey refused. Britain wanted to retain 'a free hand' ('I did not think we could give a promise of neutrality on that condition alone'). Would he agree if Germany were to guarantee the integrity of both France and her colonies? No.' - Georg Brandes *Farbenblinde Neutralität,* Zurich 1916 [15]

30 US President Woodrow Wilson, March 1919

'We know for a certainty that if Germany had thought for a moment that Great Britain would go in with France and Russia, she would never have undertaken the enterprise.'

31   Rudolf Steiner, December 1616

Let me merely remark, that certain things happened from which the only sensible conclusion to be drawn later turned out to be the correct one, namely that behind those who were in a way the puppets there stood in

32 Poster: Remember Belgium

---

[15] Quoted in Steiner, *Karma of Untruthfulness*, p.18. Brandes was Danish.

England **a powerful and influential group of people who pushed matters doggedly towards a war with Germany and through whom the way was paved for the world war that had always been prophesied.** For of course the way can be paved for what it is intended should happen. ..it is impossible to avoid realising how powerful was the group who like an outpost of mighty impulses, stood behind the puppets in the foreground. These latter are of course, perfectly honest people, yet they are puppets, and now they will vanish into obscurity.   *The Karma of Untruthfulness* Vol.1, p84.

33 Bernard Shaw on Belgium

'The violation of Belgian neutrality by the Germans was the mainstay of our righteousness; and we played it off on America for much more than it was worth. I guessed that when the German account of our dealings with Belgium reached the United states, backed with an array of facsimiles of secret diplomatic documents discovered by them in Brussels, it would be found that our own treatment of Belgium was as little compatible with neutrality as the German invasion.

34 Belgian 'invasion'

3 August: Germany offered Belgium friendly neutrality if German troops were offered safe passage.
'Germany would, by necessity, have to cross Belgium in its defence against France. Such temporary use of a right of way…There were precedents: during the Boer War, British troops were permitted passage across neutral Portuguese territory to fight in South Africa.'

- Hidden History, p. 326

36 Aftermath: the lies emerge

'As passions cooled after the war, the gigantic lies created by Great Britain's and America's propaganda were one by one exposed to the light.
'The one true and perfectly authenticated 'atrocity' in the World War, and the situation which produced by far the greatest suffering and death among the civilian population was the illegal blockade of Germany,

continued for many months after the armistice'.
- Stewart Ross, *Propaganda for War 2009,* pp.24,47

37 An Ardent Anglophile on the Error that led to War

'No sacrifice should have been too great for winning England's willingness. We should have renounced colonies and sea power, and spared English industry our competition. Only an absolutely clear orientation could lead to such a goal: renunciation of world trade and colonies; renunciation of a German war fleet; concentration of all the state's instruments of power on the land army. The result to be sure would have been a momentary limitation but a great and mighty future.'
- Hitler, *Mein Kampf* (1925)

38 The Engine of Propaganda

'...Britain's propaganda machine, an infernal engine created in war, but impossible to switch off in peace.'

'The indelible memory of atrocity stories that had taken place only in the imaginations of British propaganda agents proved to be stronger and more persistent than any facts. This curious discovery, the power of myths over facts, was the real legacy of the First World War.'   -   Richard Milton, *Best of Enemies,* 2007, p.68.

PART II OF 'HOW BRITAIN INITIATED BOTH WORLD WARS'

* * *

WORLD WAR TWO

AGAIN WE LOOK AT THE IDEA of who wanted to start a world war. This might be too disturbing: if it is, we don't want to cause any breach of the peace, so we'll just back off and just have a chat, if anybody finds what I'm going to say now too disturbing: because, we're all heavily programmed with this - the ultimate good guy Winston Churchill, Man of the Century, and the ultimate bad guy Adolf Hitler. I'm not concerned with judgments about who's good and who's bad here. We're trying to talk about the idea of wanting a war to start. This is not the history of the war, it's the process of initiation.

In 1936, Bomber Command comes into existence and long-range bombers start to be constructed. Spaight of the Air Ministry explained: "The whole raison d'etre of Bomber Command was to bomb Germany, should she be our enemy."[16] [See slide No.1] So if you believe that wars happen in accordance with the technology that exists, the manufacturing of these long-range bombers indicates some new intention - *Bomber Command* by Max Hastings says, the Lancasters were "heavy bombers which no other country in the world could match" and Germany and France had lighter bombers, primarily for air-support. They didn't build planes with the intention of bombing cities - whereas British planes could fly high and drop their bombs, and had a long range. This begins in 1936.

---

[16] J.M. Spaight, *Bombing Vindicated*, 1944, 60; N.K. *How Britain Initiated City Bombing,* CODOH.

While researching my book[17], I came across quite a lot of statements by Jews about the fact that a World War was going to happen, a war against Germany. We all know that Jews declared economic warfare against Germany in 1933, and I'm not being judgmental - what Hitler had written in *Mein Kampf*, you can appreciate that they'd be annoyed. But as well as this, there are statements that a war is going to come: "Hitler will have no war, but we will force it on him, not this year but soon" and "We will trigger a spiritual and material war of all the world against Germany" and "Our Jewish interests demand the complete destruction of Germany." [3] You might say that no truer words were ever spoken in the 20th century – that country's breeding and reproduction rate is presently at a low level which cannot possibly recover, and it may be inevitable now that German culture will fade away. So it's "a spiritual and material war" that is here blueprinted, and we may reflect on what happened at Nuremberg, when monstrous accusation were formulated against Germany, after it had been pulverised and destroyed.

Later on, when war was declared, we get statements like these: "Israeli people around the world declare economic and financial war, holy war against Hitler's people" and "Even if we Jews are not bodily with you in the trenches, we are nevertheless with you. This is our war, and you are fighting it for us" - in other words, the Jews are glad to have the goyim fighting each other one

---

[17] N.K., *Breaking the Spell, the Holocaust Myth and Reality* 2014

more time. There is a frightening book by a Tory MP Captain Archibald Ramsey called *The Nameless War* - which you might find hard to get - and he was put in jail throughout the war by Churchill, for his anti-war activity, and he said: "International Judaism has demonstrated by the course of the 20th century, that it could start a war" and destroy Germany, by a "spiritual and material war." [5] That obviously is very politically incorrect view. But if you ask, Who in the 1930s wanted another war, when nearly all the world was praying desperately that it should not happen? you do find these sources.

After the Treaty of Versailles, Germany was kind of chopped up, the peoples who felt they were German had been separated into different nations, like a jellyfish chopped up into different bits, and they were wanting to come together again, the different bits were wanting to reconnect. At Nuremberg it was declared, that these were *wars of aggression*, when Hitler went into different countries -they said he invaded Austria, he invaded Czechoslovakia and he invaded Poland. But, I want to try and put a different point of view here: these were Germanic people who were German and wanted to re-join Germany. When the German troops went into Austria, they were greeted with flowers being thrown in their path, and there was no military action, there was rejoicing, and I believe the same happened when they went into the Sudetenland, which was a part of Czechoslovakia, that they were greeted by people

who wanted to be part of Germany. Germany had been

immensely successful in the 1930s, with its prodigious economic recovery, and that became a motive for peoples wanting to be a part of Germany.

There was division around Danzig between people who felt they were German, in land that had been given to Poland. This became a terrible provocation which soon led to the war. There was a policy enunciated at Chatham House, which one could argue was being pursued by Germany.[8] After WW1, Britain and America had been talking about the right of determination of small nations, self-determination, that was a kind of mantra, and the Americans especially liked it as their formula for dismantling the British Empire -the right of self-determination of small nations. People were trying to think of, what had been the point of the first World War? Ah yes, it was Belgium's right of self-determination. Could that formula also be applied to, say, Austria, or to German-speaking people in different countries? Let's hear what was said by Lord Lothian, who addressed Chatham House in 1927:

> If the principle of self-determination were applied on behalf of Germany, in the way that it was applied against them, it would mean the re-entry of Austria into Germany, the union of Sudetenland, Danzig, and of Memel and at least certain adjustments of Poland and Silesia in the Corridor.

The key question here is, did Germans, people who feel they are German, have a right to gather together into one country? This was what Hitler called the 'Reich,' the idea of that togetherness, that would be larger than what was originally defined as Germany in 1871. Did they have that right - or, would that threaten other European countries? That is here the question. Let's focus especially on what happened to Poland in 1939. Land had been ripped away from Germany by the Treaty of Versailles at the end of the war, and given to Poland. What was defined as Poland had at most 50% of native Polish people in it, and they were trying to assert a national identity, very much by getting rid of people who they felt were outsiders, and this was having catastrophic consequences.

The historian A.J.P. Taylor said, "Danzig was the most justified of German grievances - a city of exclusively German population, which wished to return to the Reich, and Hitler himself restrained only with difficulty".[9] Germany asked: Can we build a railway and road connecting Germany with Danzig? Poland did not even reply.

Britons were concerned about German expansion, they said, you're grabbing this and you're grabbing that, and so the fatal war-guarantee was given to Poland. That led to even more truculent behavior by Poland, once Chamberlain had given it his unconditional war-guarantee.

In A.J.P. Taylor's view, there had been *no intention* to invade Poland - I think that's important. [9] Everyone nowadays believes in Hitler's bad faith, but he said, with the Czechoslovak deal, that was his last demand for land. He didn't intend to go into Poland. I want to suggest that - or rather, A.J.P. Taylor is saying that - he wanted Germany and Poland to remain on good terms.

We recall that a non-aggression pact had been signed in 1934 between Germany and Poland. Here the philosophy was, that in the last war, there had been mutual defence agreements all round Europe that had somehow flipped over to become offensive. Countries signed up to what they said was a defensive agreement, and it all went horribly wrong. So, Germany and Poland instead tried to make a non-aggression pact, which was valid for ten years. It was simply a promise, we will not invade each other. At that time, the Polish army was much bigger than the German army. That was alright, until Poland had a change in chancellor in the mid-thirties, who rejected that and took a totally different view as we'll see.

The land in question grabbed by Poland had traditionally been German land - militarily-governed by Poland long after the truce in 1918, to the newly-made state of Poland. So what was regarded as German aggression and the cause of WW2 - going into Poland - you could say this was just traditional German land being taken back. The non-aggression pact that Germany and Poland made did not allow any reporting of Polish atrocities against minority Germans. That caused the emigration of a million Germans. This is a story which you'll generally find missed-out of history books: the fate of Germans living in what had become Poland, since the Treaty of Versailles.

Late in 1938 Hitler made this offer to Poland [11], - it

would have guaranteed its boundaries and protected it against Soviet Russia. It had the German free state of Danzig given a road and rail connection, as it desired to be a part of Germany. And then - this is a bit more controversial - a plebiscite would be given to West Prussia, as to who they wanted to belong to. Poland is guaranteed an open sea-port, and they would then continue with the non-aggression pact. Poland didn't respond to that deal at all - very truculent behavior. My understanding - which you may disagree with – is that a hundred thousand Germans had to flee to the woods; or be under shelling from Polish troops from over the borders; "more than seventy thousand refugees had to be housed in German refugee camps. The aggression against Germans increased on a daily basis." [11]

It may be hard to believe this, but Poland was *wanting* war with Germany. [14] It published a map of Europe showing a whole lot of Germany carved out and having become Poland. This became far worse when in March, 1939, Chamberlain gave this unconditional war-guarantee to Poland. It had had a non-aggression pact with Germany, and that was rejected, and instead there was a war-guarantee: which said that in any war with Germany, *even if Poland starts it,* Britain would come in. That was just what Poland wanted because it did want war.

Poland intensified its persecution of the German minority. Speaking German in public was prosecuted - this is land that had been German, up until 1918. German-associated newspapers were suppressed, and so forth. The Germans felt this nullified the agreement which they had made at Munich in September 1938 for Britain and Germany to work closely together to maintain the peace.

Chamberlain had felt he wanted to do something, but what was he going to do? Buchanan in his *The Unnecessary War* tends to regard it as the most foolish act of statesmanship in British history - the war-guarantee given to Poland. People just couldn't believe that Britain had done such a thing. I recommend that book as the best possible analysis of this catastrophic moment, which precipitated the truculent Polish behavior.

When we look back at the way the war broke out, we may wonder, could not Germany have just done nothing for a few years? After all, Czechoslovakia and Austria, weren't they enough? Couldn't it have just stayed that way, just left it, left the Danzig problem, just let everything calm down - couldn't it have just done nothing?

Well, let us suppose there were people who wanted war - if we suppose that - once that British war-guarantee had been given, all they had to do was intensify the persecution of Germans in that part of Poland, until Germany had to do something about it. So, here is a German view I've got - and it's difficult to get a German view on the subject, isn't it? You hardly get books translated from the German available. I got this from a website[18] - 'The British promise to wage war

---

[18] William J. Scott *Deutsche Staatszeitung*, March 20, 2010

against Germany, if only Poland would succeed to get Germany into the war, even by aggression' - so Poland's rabid incitement against Germany was escalated, Polish newspapers demand the occupation of Danzig, all of East Prussia, they advocate Poland should push its border all the way to the river, maybe annexing Berlin. They felt they'd got the superior army, and this was kind of truculent behavior, and the new President of Poland said (1939) "Poland wants war with Germany, and Germany will not be able to avoid it, even if she wants to".

That was true enough. Poland seems to have thought that a cavalry charge could somehow manage against the German tanks. Nobody quite knew how … yes?

> Audience comment: …'Roosevelt was on the phone continually in this pre-war period, encouraging the Poles to act intransigently.'[19] Yes thank you for that.

You will not readily find that in the history books, for example this one, [*The Unnecessary War,* Buchanan] excellent though it is, gives no accounts of the open terror, murder and rape in the months preceding September '39. This may be something where one has to get so-called 'far-right' Revisionist books [i.e., books that will attend to Germany's viewpoint] to find a mention. On my understanding that is why Germany

---

[19] ihr.org, Mark Weber, 'President Roosevelt's Campaign to Incite War in Europe, The Secret Polish Documents.'

had to do something, had to take some sort of action.

Here's a British ex-pat giving a testimony[20]:[15] "Terrorists began murdering civilians in large numbers. On the nights of August 25th to August 31, that is just days before the war, there are authenticated acts of armed violence against German officials and property. These incidents took place on the border or inside German territory." So, deliberate provocation was going on. "Mobs were assaulting thousands of men, women and children" – so Germany was I would suggest coming to the rescue of these Germans who were being done in.

On August 30th, Poland orders total mobilisation – under the Protocols of the League of Nations, that is equivalent to a declaration of war[21]. [17] One could argue that it was Poland that effectively declared war and Germany had to respond. Germany then goes in, at the beginning of September, to the pre-Versailles German areas given to Poland. Was that aggression? I'm saying that there was a reason for Germany having to do this, and that it was not part of the original plan. They had originally asked for Danzig to be returned, for a connection to be made with Danzig. If England had wanted to avoid the war, it could have leant on Poland, to give some sort of rights to the German minorities there. And, it could have leant on Poland to agree to a

[20] http://tomatobubble.com/id570.html William Joyce *Twilight over England*
[21] On mobilisation as legally signifying war, see *Hidden History*, p.278.

railway being built. I'd have thought that these were reasonable demands, that if Anglo-German friendship had been desired, that could have been done, as far as I can see, to remove this immediate cause of war.

Germany thought that by going in with the Soviet Union, that would somehow not activate the British guarantee to Poland – that, with those two going in together, Britain would not declare war on both of them.

Upon entering Danzig, the German army are *showered with flowers.* Here is a comment from a German commander, about that reception. "It was like this everywhere – in the Rhineland, in Vienna, in the Sudeten territories and in Memel – do you still doubt the mission of the Fuhrer?" [18] That is greatly missed out from modern accounts, that there was rejoicing amongst the German people, when a connection was made with the motherland of Germany.

At Nuremberg, these were described as *wars of aggression* – he's gone in here, he's gone in there, but another way of looking at it, is that there were different populations who felt they were German wanting to live together and wanting to be together, and the whole Second World War was about that *not* being permitted. No, that greater expanse of Europe, of people wanting to be German together, cannot be permitted.

Here is as it were the greater Germany that tried to come together, [19] and everybody decided it could not be allowed. Czechoslovakia was very outrageously occupied. Hitler went into Prague – that was (I suggest) the terrible, catastrophic error that he made, of going into Prague where he had no business to be. Czechoslovakia (1918-1993) was what we would nowadays call a failed state. It was coming apart in 1938. It was patched together in the Treaty of Versailles from divers bits of Europe that didn't want to be together. Instead of just saying, this is outrageous German aggression, we could say, Sudetenland wanted to be part of Germany, and likewise the Poles in Czechoslovakia wanted to be part of Poland. So it kind of broke up. I may not be defending what the Germans did, of going into Czechoslovakia.

France invaded Germany on September 7th, to eight kilometres. We're always told how wicked it is for Germany to have occupied France, so let's just point out that France did invade Germany a week after Britain declared war.

I want to look at the subject of German peace-offers, I think this is relevant to the question of who was responsible for the war and who started the war. Possibly the best book on the subject is *Himmler's Secret War* by Martin Allen – I had quite a bit to do with investigating this book.[22] It describes the cascade of German peace-offers that kept appearing, right through the war[23], and how Churchill first of all forbade anyone

---

22 N.K.,, The "Ministry of Truth" at Britain's National Archives: The Attempt to Discredit Martin Allen, *Inconvenient History*, 2014, 6.

[23] '… sixteen German peace offers in the first two years of the Second world War' – Martin Allen, *Himmler's Secret War,*

to look at them, and then, towards the end of 1940 the British black-ops started to use the peace offers, to manipulate Germany, by making them think they would take them seriously, while actually they just wanted the appearance of using them for purposes of deception.

Let's have a quote. Hitler said, "I've always expressed to France my desire to bury forever our ancient enmity, and bring together these two nations, both of which have such glorious pasts... I have devoted no less effort to an achievement of Anglo-German understanding, no more than that, of Anglo-German friendship. At no time and at no place have I ever acted contrary to British interests... *Why should this war in the West be fought*?" [21] Two main German peace-offers came in October 1939 and July 1940, both dismissed by Britain.

Are you surprised if I say that Hitler always had a deep admiration for Britain, always wanted friendship with Britain, is that surprising? Hitler's *Mein Kampf* was totally banned during the War, because it had a major theme, of the tremendous importance of good relations with Britain. He would watch films of say the British in India, and he would say, there, that's the master-race, that's what the master-race was like. If I may quote Richard Milton's fine book, *Best of Enemies*: "The leader of the resurgent German nation and the Nazi party was a self-professed Anglophile, whose primary foreign– policy aim was an alliance with Britain." [22] This may remind us of the Kaiser yearning for a deal of friendship

the covert peace negotiations of Heinrich Himmler, 2014, p.55.

that could never happen.

Let's quote from David Irving, his *Hitler's War.* (His first book on Dresden had been an international bestseller). He was well-known, respected and liked, and then he did ten years' research on *Hitler's War*, using original sources, from people who know him and so forth, and again it sold rather well - but Macmillan pulped all his books and he suddenly found himself *persona non grata*. Anyway here's a quote from him. Rudolf Hess asked him, '"Mein Fuhrer, are your views about the British still the same?" Hitler gloomily sighed, "If only the British knew how *little* I ask of them." How he liked to leaf through the glossy pages of *Tatler,* studying the British aristocracy in their natural habitat! Once he was overheard to say, "Those are valuable specimens, those are the ones I'm going to make peace with"'. [23] So he was scheming how to make peace with Britain, but he never quite made it.

Terrific non-stop fantasizing goes on about Germany having wanted to invade Britain. I see the magazine *History Today* this week has got a big item on it. The British were being given gas masks etc to prepare for when this wicked man would come to take over our country. If I may quote two quite respected sources [24]: Sir Basil Hart, *Revolution in Warfare*, and History of 2nd World War- There was "a but faintly imagined and conditional plan to invade Britain in the summer of 1940". Basically, they just wanted to get up to Biggin Hill and stop the bombers taking off. I suggest that any desire to invade Britain was motivated by a desire to stop those bomber planes taking off, that were incinerating the cities of Germany. Also, "At no time did this man Hitler pose or intend a real threat to Britain or to the Empire" - that was David Irving's view, that I suggest we should accept.

A.J.P. Taylor, the renowned historian, has well described the Second World War in which sixty million people died as "Less wanted by nearly everybody than almost any other war in history." Was it *even less* wanted than the First World War? We here pose the question, who wants it to happen, who makes it happen? Once again Winston Churchill was the First Sea-Lord, the same position as he held in the First World War. Initially he held that position, then he became Prime Minister.

We listen to his Reasons for War, as to why there should be another war with Germany. Back in November 1936 he said: "Germany is becoming too powerful, we have to crush it". That's years before any war breaks out. David Irving discovered – unhappily for his reputation – that the group Focus was set up in 1936 by the Chair of the Board of Jewish Deputies, basically Churchill's bills. [27] As a membership group, 'The Anti-Nazi League', or the Focus, it promoted and supported Churchill, and its imperative was – quoting David Irving – "first of all, the tune that Churchill had to play was, fight Germany". Churchill's debts from gambling and heavy boozing – and he had been a hospitalized alcoholic, let's bear that in mind – all his bills for brandy would be paid, and his stately home would not be auctioned off, thanks to this group, The Focus.

Let's have a few more of Churchill's Reasons for War. In 1939, "This war is an English war, and its goal is the destruction of Germany". What kind of war-aim is that? Normally wars are fought for some land-purpose, or because you are annoyed, or somebody has insulted you, or you need some raw materials. But no - this is a goal which does not permit any negotiation. Diplomats cannot resolve this, if the guy in charge says the goal is the destruction of Germany - this being the mightiest nation in the centre of Europe, this being the Christian heart of Europe. The two strongest nations in Europe inevitably are going to be Britain and Germany, because they have got the iron and coal underneath the ground. They are inevitably the strongest. Anyone who wants to foster war between Britain and Germany, can only be wanting the destruction of Europe, or the undermining and disintegration of Europe, that's (I suggest) the only possible motive.

Then Churchill said, "You must understand, this war is not against Hitler or National Socialism, but against the strength of the German people, which is to be smashed once and for all." [28] What kind of statement is that? I suggest that you will not find in the utterances of Winston Churchill, any trace of ethics or morality. This is the Man of the Century and it's just my interpretation. Again Churchill: "The war is not just a matter of elimination of fascism in Germany, but rather about obtaining German sales markets." Huh? Then again: "Germany's unforgiveable crime before WW2 was its attempt to loosen its economy from out of the world trade system and build up an independent exchange system from which the world finance could not profit any more." The ever-glorious achievement of Nazi Germany in the 1930s was to manage its own banking system, away from the tentacles of Rothschild control. It printed its own money at source, that's why it had that terrific economic recovery, that no other European country could match. No other country before or since in Europe managed that in the 20th century, escaping from the clutches of international bankers. Churchill is seeing that as a Reason for War.

Those are the reasons given by Churchill, which you may or may not find much sense in.

He gets elected on May 10th ,and on the next day May 11th city bombing begins. This is the most terrible crime ever conceived by the mind of man, to ignite cities full of people. How can anyone be so wicked as to want to do such a thing? It begins with cities like Hamburg, Duesberg, and these are not reported in the British newspapers. Let's hear from an important philosophical book by Veale, *Advance to Barbarism, the Development of Total Warfare:* "The raid on the night of May 11th, 1940, was an epoch-making event, since it was the first deliberate breach of the fundamental rule of civilized warfare, that hostilities must only be waged against enemy-combatant forces." You don't hear a lot about this in official accounts of the war.

> Floor comment about German bombing of the Spanish town Guernica in 1930s. It was less than a hundred deaths, Communists were retreating, I don't think that's in any way comparable to what's happening here.

This then continues, with Churchill wanting to provoke Hitler to return the bombing, and he's frustrated that it doesn't happen. Starting on May 11th, there was a pretence that it was against the Ruhr's industrial targets, but actually the planes are flying high, dropping their bombs whenever they see the lights of a city - it is city-bombing. AJP Taylor was a brilliant and very successful historian, who could never ever get to lecture at Oxford University again, after these words of his were published: "The almost universal belief that Hitler started the indiscriminate bombing of civilians, whereas it was started by the directors of British strategy, as some of the more honest among them have boasted." To what was he alluding? The first carpet-bombing of a German city was Duesberg on 15th May, followed by Hamburg on the 16th, as *not* reported in British newspapers. The British people don't know this is happening, that is my impression.

Churchill defines the point of the war in the House of Commons on May 13th, as Britain's new Prime Minister. He says "our aim, in one word is victory, victory at all costs". [32] What could victory mean, over a country that has never ever wanted to fight Britain, always wanted friendship with Britain? It's triggered by Poland, a country that did not then exist, having been swallowed up by Germany and the Soviet Union, so what would victory mean? Victory I suggest means what he has earlier defined, viz. the destruction of Germany. I suggest that is the war-aim that is implied, when he says victory at all costs. What he here means by victory, implies that any negotiation is pointless. There's nothing to negotiate about, he just wants to smash Germany. I would suggest that Churchill's foreign policy is fully expressed in three words, *wreck, smash, destroy*. That's just a personal impression of course. He gets a thrill out of all this. He's very good at organizing. He creates the terrific fantasy - which British people still believe to this day - that a monstrous fiend wanted to invade this island. Why? Because it wanted world-domination. That is the 'evil monster' he was fighting against – which Britons still believe, to this day.

What happened at Dunkirk has, for the first time, appeared into a mainstream book [Buchanan, *The Unnecessary War*] – before that it had been just a few weirdo revisionists who believed it.[24] The British army had been totally routed and was cornered on the beaches of Dunkirk. It was totally at the mercy of the German troops, who were about to wipe them out, and then suddenly an order came from the top level, to stop. No, you're not allowed to wipe out these British troops? Why not? The generals didn't believe it, they said, this must be a mistake. And they started to close in, then another order came. Then Hitler himself turned up. [33]

Here was the most terrible row that Hiltler had with Rudolf Hess, his chief advisor and soul-mate in all of this. Hess said, for God's sake go in, you've got to wipe them out, it's the only way, if you want to win the war.

---

[24] But see also the British account of 2001: 'The miracle' of Dunkirk', in *Double Standards, The Rudolf Hess cover-up*, by Lynn Pickett, Clive Prince and Stephen Prior, pp.116-120.

And he said, 'No, I will not do it, I will not attack these British troops'. Why not? Let's read what he said. Here is one report, of an astounded general having Hitler himself lecturing him. "He, Hitler, astonished us by speaking with admiration of the British Empire" – this is at Dunkirk, right? "Of the necessity for its existence, and of the civilization that Britain had brought into the world. He compared the British Empire with the Catholic Church." The two institutions he admired most in the world were the Catholic Church and the British Empire, as being forces for stability. The things he hated most were the Bolsheviks and international finance. "He compared the British Empire with the Catholic Church, they were both essential elements of stability in the world. All he wanted from Britain, was that she should acknowledge Germany's position on the Continent. The return of Germany's colonies would be desirable but not essential, and he would offer to support Britain with troops if she should be involved in difficulties anywhere."

I believe that the Kaiser did that too – both Kaiser and Hitler made the offer, that they would be happy to lend German troops in support, should there be anywhere that the British Empire needed support. In WW2 Britain had a very clear choice, of Germany in favour of the British Empire and supporting it, and praising it and admiring it, whereas America had a clear policy of breaking up the British Empire because it wanted its own. That was a very clear choice Britain had, whom to ally with.

Here is another astonished general remembering from

Dunkirk, who had Hitler explaining to him why Brits stranded on the beach there should not be wiped out, but instead they should all be allowed to return to England. [34] He cherished the vain and absurd hope that this would lead to some sort of friendship or acceptance of a deal for ending the war. But instead, Churchill just made up his own story about it, and it was more or less forgotten. Hitler had then explained: "The blood of every single Englishman is too valuable to be shed … Our two people belong together racially and traditionally. This is and always has been my aim." We are Anglo-Saxons and the Germans are Saxons. How is it possible that we should be fighting each other?

Floor comment – Speak for yourself, I am Celtic.

This is at the end of May when Churchill has come into power, and has initiated the bombing of German cities. So this Dunkirk episode happens – I feel there is a contrast here of sanity and madness – with Hitler saying that Germany and Britain should never fight each other, and wanting some kind of friendship. What he was up against was what we may call the 'Phantom Menace,' the demonised enemy image: here is the arch-fiend who wants world-domination and so on. We can't do a deal, and Germans are so wicked that we've just got to bomb their cities - the most unbelievably horrific concept.

Here is a chap who worked for the British Air Ministry. He is explaining – and there aren't many books which frankly describe how the RAF started bombing cities - the "Strategic Bombing Offensive." [35] Quoting from his book called *Bombing Vindicated*: "We have shrunk from giving our great decision of May 11th the publicity which it deserved." He explained that Hitler had not wanted the mutual bombing to go on: "Again and again the German official reports applauded the reprisal elements in the actions of the Luftwaffe ... If you stop bombing us, we'll stop bombing you." To this day, British people do not believe that, do they? They will admire the heroism of the Battle of Britain and the Blitz, but will not believe that a peace offer was always on the table: If you stop bombing us, we'll stop bombing you. This one-sided bombing of German cities went on for three whole months, before the Germans responded. The Luftwaffe finally bombed London, on September 6th.

Peace-leaflets were dropped over London in June 1940, called "an appeal to reason," quoting Hitler that, "I can see no reason why this war must go on" [34]. He talked about the enemy who "for the second time has declared war upon us for no reason whatever." A crucial moment when Churchill killed the peace offensive in England, Irving said, was July 1940.

Here is a quote from *Mein Kampf* showing Hitler's admiration of Britain, of what he sees as the tough quality of the British people, whereby they got their empire. [Slide 38].

What we might call David Irving's thesis, as I'm not aware of any other historian who has backed this up, has British city-bombing start on 11th May and that carries on, with massive bombing of Berlin for example

65

in August as a hundred planes go over and start bombing Berlin, repeatedly, whereas only on the 6th September does the Luftwaffe come and bomb London. Then East London goes up in flames, and Churchill finally gets what he wants. At last he can sit back and enjoy another lovely war! He leaves London whenever he gets intelligence in advance that the bombing is going to come. He is perfectly safe, then returns the next morning and wanders round, greeting people amidst the wreckage of their homes. They say, Good old Winnie, we knew you'd stand by us!

He has brought on the bombing of London by this manipulation. Let's be aware that, as Prime Minister, he can simply ring up Bomber Command: 'I want a hundred bombers go over to Berlin' – he doesn't have to go through Parliament or anything. It is staggering and horrific that a Prime Minister can do that, can more or less get a war going of his own initiative. On what one might call David Irving's thesis, Luftwaffe that drop bombs on London town are reprimanded, because only military targets are allowed, and that is a strict policy; whereas *by mistake*, on August 24th, some bombers go too far and drop stuff on London - that mistake enables the big response, that Churchill wants. That is Irving's theme which seems quite likely.

This is just echoing what we have just said, a peace message did come through from Sweden, Victor Mallett [39] and the War Cabinet gave instructions to ignore it.

What was called the Blitz began on the 6th September, when the Luftwaffe set East London alight. Let me quote a great modern revisionist Arthur Butz, in *The Hoax of the 20th Century* (1976): "The British people were not permitted to find out that the government could have stopped the German raids at any time, merely by stopping the raids on Germany." [41] People are thrilled by the suffering, with the Blitz being regarded as our finest hour, 'We survived the Blitz.' One should rather ask people, Why did you want to have that? What was the point of bombing Germany so that you could have a Blitz in London? Was it just so

Churchill could enjoy his war, or was there some other purpose, apart from devastating cities in Europe?

Image: The Blitz

Peace offers were coming though the King of Sweden, through the Pope, all sorts of people were giving these, all being ignored. Let me cite one of these, in November

1940. [43] This one was so good it was quite difficult for the British government to ignore it:

- All these countries in Europe – Norway, Denmark, Holland, Belgium, France to be independent and free states.
- The political independence and national identity of a Polish state to be restored – remember Poland had been swallowed up. So Germany would do its bit to restore it, it couldn't do anything about what Russia had.
- Czechoslovakia would not be prevented from developing her national character" – so if there were bits of Czechoslovakia that wanted to be together, Germany would not prevent that.
- It would like some German colonies restored, and greater European economic solidarity to be pursued.

That was the crux of this offer that came in November 1940. His book has been very much attacked and denounced by the British establishment, and Martin Allen, I surmise he's been bumped off actually, or he is no longer around. We tried to contact him, after he came out with this book and they tried to discredit it, by claiming that letters he used in the National Archive were forged – I won't go into all that – but I don't think he's around anymore.[25] He described this as "a peace offer so generous that it left most of Britain's war aims sounding utterly hollow." This rather refutes, I suggest, the idea that Germany sought world-domination. I think that is rather refuted. Such peace offers being just dismissed may tend to show, who wanted the war.

---

[25] See refs 21,22.

Two million tons of bombs were dropped in this ghastly process, reducing to rubble the wonderful cultural heritage of Europe - by Britain and America. People say, how terrible, what the Nazis did to Coventry, how wicked! [45] But they never appreciate the ratio of tonnage of bombs dropped by each side, a *twenty-to-one* ratio: the tonnage of bombs dropped on Germany, compared to what they dropped on Britain. Here's an analysis of it, showing a mere five percent of total bombs dropped fell on Britain.

David Irving argued that what happened with the attack on Warsaw was not comparable to what Britain did with city bombing: then, notice was given, leaflets were dropped warning the civilian population, and every effort was made, I think, to resolve the situation amicably before war broke out. Then a formal ultimatum was given. Bombardment of a city is allowed under these conditions under the Hague Conventions. [46] I would say that Germany fought both wars in accord with the Hague Conventions, which you can't say for this country.

I'm asking you the question really, we've looked at two different world wars, do you feel there was anything in common regarding the way they were initiated and the motives for them? Have I completely distorted things in saying that Germany didn't want these wars and was very much the victim?

* * * * * **

SLIDES USED

1 Bomber command

1936: 'Bomber Command' comes into existence, and long-range bomber planes start to be constructed. Its purpose was candidly described by J.M.Spaight of the Air Ministry: 'The whole *raison d'etre* of Bomber Command was to bomb Germany should she be our enemy.' So, those who wanted war started planning for it.

2 Plans for City Bombing

The Lancasters were 'heavy bombers which no other country in the world could match.' Germany and France had lighter bombers 'primarily for air support,' or 'tactical air power.'   Max Hastings, *Bomber Command* 1979, 50.

3 Jews Declare War

"We Jews are going to bring a war on Germany." D.A. Brown, National Chairman, United Jewish Campaign,1934

"Hitler will have no war (does not want war), but we will force it on him, not this year, but soon"   Emil Ludwig

Cohn in *Les Annales,* June 1934

'We will trigger a spiritual and material war of all the world against Germany's ambitions to become once again a great nation, to recover lost territories and colonies. But our Jewish interests demand the complete destruction of Germany.' - Vladimir Jabotinsky (founder of terror group, Irgun Zvai Leumi) in *Mascha Rjetsch*, January 1934

4 "The Israeli people around the world declare economic and financial war against Germany... holy war against Hitler's people."   8 Sept 1939, *Jewish Chronicle*, declared by Chaim Weizmann, the Zionist leader

"Even if we Jews are not bodily with you in the trenches, we are nevertheless morally with you. This is OUR WAR, and you are fighting it for us." —*Les Nouvelles Litteraires*, 10 February 1940

5 Captain Ramsey's View

 "International Judaism has demonstrated by the course of the 20th century that it could start war" and destroy Germany by "a spiritual and material war." - Tory MP Captain Archibald Ramsay, *The Nameless War (1952)*

Captain Ramsey

7 <u>Chatham House policy, 1927</u>

German policy adhered closely to the opinions of **Lord Lothian** in an address in 1927 at Chatham House said: **"Now, if the principle of self-determination were applied on behalf of Germany, in the way that it was applied against them, it would mean the re-entry of Austria into Germany, the union of Sudetenland, Danzig, and probably Memel with Germany and at least certain adjustments with Poland in Silesia and in the Corridor"** - Fish, H., *FDR: The Other Side of the Coin*, 1976, p108

6 Germany after Versailles

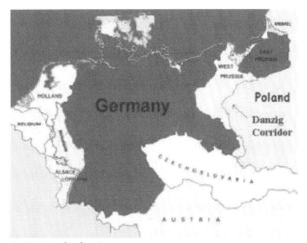

9 A.J.P. Taylor's view

... Danzig was the most justified of German grievances: a city of exclusively German population which manifestly wished to return to the Reich and which Hitler himself restrained only with difficulty...
The destruction of Poland had been no part of his original project. On the contrary, he had wished to solve the question of Danzig so that Germany and Poland could remain on good terms..." *Origin of 2nd WW*

8 Polish 'corridor'

10 Polish border

The "Peace Makers" in Versailles granted most of the German land militarily conquered by Poland long after the truce in 1918 to the newly made state of Poland. Under the nonaggression treaty German newspapers were not allowed to report on Polish atrocities against the minority Germans, which led to the emigration of a million Germans.

11 Offer to Poland October 1938

- Guarantee of its boundaries, even to protect it against Soviet Russia.
- Return of the German free State of Danzig, with road & rail connection
- Plebiscite to be given to West Prussia. Poland

gets open-sea port

- Extend polish-German non-aggression pact

Polish Response: a hundred thousand Germans had to flee to the woods, or, under shelling from Polish soldiers, over the borders. Between March and August more than 70.000 refugees had to be housed in German refugee camps & the aggression against Germans increased on a daily basis.

12 British War-Guarantee

The British war-guarantee of 31 March 1939 gave Poland carte blanche in its dealings with Germany. Poland intensified its persecutions of the German minority. Abductions became common, speaking German in public was proscribed, German associations and newspapers were suppressed, the German consul in Krakow was murdered, etc.

This nullified the Munich agreement of September 1938 for Britain & Germany to work closely together to avoid war; also the Polish-German-Polish Declaration of non-aggression (1934).

13 Effect of British war-guarantee

The British promised to wage war against Germany, if only Poland would succeed to get Germany into the war, even by aggression! This immediately escalated Poland's rabid incitement against Germany. **Polish**

newspapers demanded the occupation of Danzig, all of east Prussia, in fact they advocated that Poland should push its border all the way to the Oder River, some again advocated the annexation of Berlin and even Hamburg - William J. Scott, *Deutsche Staatszeitung*, March 20, 2010

14 Poles demand war

"Poland wants war with Germany and Germany will not be able to avoid it even if she wants to." - Poland's President Edward Rydz-Smigly, *Daily Mail*, August 6th, 1939.[26]

The German minority had been disfranchised in the 1920s, and in the 1930s it was subjected to open terror, murder and rape, especially in the months preceding September 1939.

15 Polish terror attacks

Terrorists begin murdering German civilians in large numbers. A British ex-Pat named William Joyce describes the events:

"On the nights of August 25 to August 31 inclusive, there occurred, besides innumerable attacks on civilians

---

[26] There is a problem with this widely-quoted remark, that 6th August was a Sunday: there was no Sunday edition of the *Mail*.

of German blood, 44 perfectly authenticated acts of armed violence against German official persons and property. These incidents took place either on the border or inside German territory.

16   Of all the crimes of World War II, one never hears about the wholesale massacres that occurred in Poland just before the war. Thousands of German men, women and children were massacred in the most horrendous fashion by press-enraged mobs. Hitler decided to halt the slaughter and he rushed to the rescue. Young German boys, when captured by the Poles, were castrated.   - Léon Degrelle

Since dawn today, we are shooting back ... A. Hitler

17   War

August 30th: Poland orders total mobilization - under the Protocols of the League of Nations this is equal to a declaration of war. Polish troops were numerically stronger

September 1940: Germany reclaimed the pre-Versailles German areas given to Poland.

H's speech at Danzig harped on the sadistic treatment of Poles to the German minorities: 'Tens of thousands were deported, maltreated, killed in the most bestial fashion.'

18   Showered with flowers

Danzig, September 1939:_ 'It was like this everywhere..
in the Rhineland, in Vienna, in the Sudetan territories,
and in Memel: do you still doubt the mission of the
Fuhrer?'   - Comment by Schmundt, Irving *Hitler's War*
p.226

20 France invades Germany
The French invade Germany on September 7th, 1939,
advancing 8 km before stopping.

21   German peace offers
 Hitler: "I have always expressed to France my desire to
bury forever our ancient enmity and bring together
these two nations, both of which have such glorious
pasts. ....I have devoted no less effort to the
achievement of Anglo-German understanding, no, more
than that, of an Anglo-German friendship. At no time
and in no place have I ever acted contrary to British
interests...**Why should this war in the West be
fought?**" 6th October. Two German peace offers to
Britain came in October 1939, after defeating Poland,
and in July 1940, after defeating France, both spurned.
-    Captain R. Grenfell, *Unconditional Hatred, German
War guilt and the Future of Europe,* NY 1954, 201

19 Map of 'Greater Germany', 1939

22 Admiration for Britain

During and after the war, it was hard to obtain an English translation of Hitler's *Mein Kampf*, 'a central theme of which was Hitler's admiration for and longing for friendship with Great Britain' - Captain Arthur Ramsey, *The Nameless War*, p. 49 (in jail through the war.)

'From the outset, the leader of the resurgent German nation and Nazi party was a self-confessed Anglophile whose primary foreign policy aim was an alliance with Britain.' - Richard Milton, *Best of Enemies*, 2007, p.169

23 An Anglophile

Early 1940, Rudolf Hess once enquired, 'Mein Fuhrer, are your views about the British still the same? Hitler gloomily sighed, ' If only the British knew how *little* I ask of them!

How he liked to leaf through the glossy pages of *The Tatler,* studying the British aristocracy in their natural habitat! Once he was overheard to say, 'Those are valuable specimens – those are the ones I am going to make peace with.'   David Irving, *Hitler's war.*

24 Invasion of UK?

'A but faintly-imagined and conditional German plan to invade Britain in the summer of 1940' - Sir Basil Liddell Hart, *The Revolution in Warfare*, 1946, pp.212-222 (see also his *History of the 2nd World War* 1970, pp.93-6)
 "the discovery.. that at no time did this man (Hitler) pose or intend a real threat to Britain or the Empire." – David Irving, foreword to his book *The Warpath* (1978)

25   Who wanted another war?

The war of 1939 was 'less wanted by nearly everybody than almost any other war in history.' - A.J.P. Taylor

27 A Reason for War

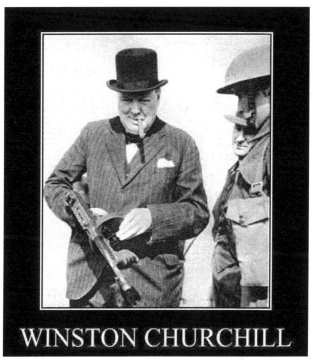

WINSTON CHURCHILL

"Germany becomes too powerful. We have to crush it." - Winston Churchill November 1936 speaking to US - General Robert E. Wood

The Churchill pressure group *The Focus* was established in 1936 by Sir Waley Cohen (Chair of the Board of Jewish Deputies) who gave fifty thousand pounds. 'The purpose was – the tune that Churchill had to play was – fight Germany' – David Irving.

28 Reasons for War – 2

"This war is an English war and its goal is the destruction of Germany." - Churchill, Autumn 1939 broadcast

"You must understand that this war is not against Hitler or National Socialism, but against the strength of the German people, which is to be smashed once and for all, regardless of whether it is in the hands of Hitler or a Jesuit priest." - Churchill (Emrys Hughes in *Winston Churchill - His Career in War and Peace*, page 145)

29 Reasons for War - 3

"The war was not just a matter of elimination of fascism in Germany, but rather obtaining German sales markets" Churchill, March 1946

"Germany's unforgivable crime before WW2 was its attempt to loosen its economy out of the world trade system and to build up an independent exchange system from which the world-finance couldn't profit anymore." -Churchill, *The Second World War* - Bern, 1960.

30 Churchill elected

Churchill ousts Chamberlain as Prime Minister on May 10th 1940, and next day the city-bombing begins.

'This raid on the night of May 11th, 1940, although in itself trivial, was an epoch-marking event since it was

the first deliberate breach of the fundamental rule of civilised warfare that hostilities must only be waged against enemy combatant forces. Veale *Advance to Barbarism, The Development of Total War,*1970, 170

For 12th May, War Cabinet minutes note on 'Bombing Policy,' that the Prime Minister was 'no longer bound by our previously-held scruples as to initiating "unrestricted" air warfare.'

31 City bombing in WW2

' ... the almost universal belief that Hitler started the indiscriminate bombing of civilians, whereas it was started by the directors of British strategy, as some of the more honest among them have boasted.' - A.J.P. Tayler*, Origins of 2nd World War,*1972, 16.

The first carpet bombing of a German city was in the night from 15 to 16 May 1940 in Duisburg; followed by repeated air attacks on German cities - bombing of Hamburg on May 16th.

32 What was the point?

Churchill, May 13th 1940: You ask, what is our aim? I can answer in one word. It is victory, victory at all costs.'

33 Dunkirk: May 1940

"He (Hitler) then astonished us by speaking with admiration of the British Empire, of the necessity for its existence, and of the civilization that Britain had brought into the world. ....He compared the British Empire with the Catholic Church saying they were both essential elements of stability in the world. He said that all he wanted from Britain was that she should acknowledge Germany's position on the Continent. The return of Germany's colonies would be desirable but not essential, and he would even offer to support Britain with troops if she should be involved in difficulties anywhere." - General Gunther von Blumentritt, at Dunkirk.

34 At Dunkirk - 2

"The blood of every single Englishman is too valuable to be shed," Hitler told his friend Frau Troost. "Our two people belong together racially and traditionally – this is and always has been my aim even if our generals can't grasp it." - Patrick Buchanan, *The Unnecessary* War, 2008, p.326.

35 Strategic Bombing Initiated

'Because we were doubtful about the psychological effect of the distortion of the truth that it was we who started the strategic bombing offensive, we have shrunk from giving our great decision of May 11th 1940 the

publicity which it deserved. That surely was a mistake.'-
J.M. Spaight, Assist. Sec. to the Air Ministry, *Bombing Vindicated 1944.*

36 German desire for peace

'Hitler assuredly did not want the mutual bombing to go on. … Again and again the German official reports applauded the reprisal element in the actions of the Luftwaffe … 'If you stop bombing us, we'll stop bombing you.' - Spaight, *Bombing Vindicated, 1944* 43.

37 Peace offer June 1940

June 1940: Luftwaffe drop "peace leaflets" over London with "an appeal to "reason". Hitler: **'I can see no reason why this war must go on.** I am grieved to think of the sacrifices it will claim. I should like to avert them. As for my own people, I know that millions of German men, young and old alike, are burning with the desire to settle accounts with the enemy who for the second time has declared war upon us for no reason whatever.' Irving: 'The crucial moment when he [Churchill] managed to kill this peace offensive in England was July 1940'

38 Praise for Albion

'England has always possessed whatever armament she

happened to need. She always fought with the weapons which success demanded. She fought with mercenaries as long as mercenaries sufficed; but she reached down into the precious blood of the whole nation when only such a sacrifice could bring victory; but the determination for victory, the tenacity and ruthless pursuit of this struggle, remained unchanged.'
Hitler, *Mein Kampf,1925*

39 From 11 May to 6 September

July 20: Prime minister Winston Churchill hears of latest German peace offer (US-to-Berlin decode) & instructs Lord Halifax to block it. He then asks Bomber Command if they can do a 'savage attack upon Berlin.'
August 24: German planes by mistake hit East London. H. issues command that any aircrew that drops bombs on London will be severely reprimanded, with only the RAF, dockyards, etc. as targets.
August 26: a hundred heavy bombers sent to hit Berlin
September 4:   (after 7 raids) Hitler formulates another peace offer => Victor Mallet in Stockholm, who replies he is 'not allowed' to hear it.
September 6:   Luftwaffe bomb London   - David Irving video, *'Churchill's War'*

40   No peace deal

'The War Cabinet instructed Mallet to ignore the

message. But it is the clearest indication that Hitler's words in Mein Kampf were not mere rhetoric. He believed profoundly that an Anglo-German alliance was essential and was prepared to go the last mile to try to conclude such an agreement. Now he was compelled to realise that there would be no negotiated peace.' - Richard Milton, *Best of Enemies,* 2007 p.222.

41 'The Blitz'

On 25 August, 81 bombers made night raids over Berlin, then on 6th September the Luftwaffe replied. Only after six surprise attacks upon Berlin in the previous fortnight did the Blitz begin, and thus Germany justifiably called it a reprisal.

'The British people were not permitted to find out that the Government could have stopped the German raids at any time merely by stopping the raids on Germany.' - Professor Arthur Butz. *The Hoax of the 20th Century,* 1976, 70

42 Image: The Blitz

43 November 1940 peace offer Via the Pope:

- *Norway, Denmark, Holland, Belgium and France to be independent free states,*
- *the political independence and national identity of a 'Polish state' to be restored*

- *Czechoslovakia would 'not be prevented from developing her national character'*
- *Some German colonies restored, etc.*
- *Greater European economic solidarity to be pursued*

'A peace offer so generous that it left most of Britain's war aims sounding utterly hollow' – Martin Allen, *Himmler's Secret War,* 2005, p.100

44 Two million tons

"Many of the most beautiful cities of Europe and the world were systematically pounded into nothingness, often during the last weeks of the war, among them: Wuerzburg, Hildesheim, Darmstadt, Kassel, Nürnberg, Braunschweig." - Dr Wesserle, *The Journal of Historical Review,* 1981, vol. 2, 381-384.

45 The 1:20 ratio, tons of bombs

Anglo-American strategic bombers dropped 2690 kilotons of bombs on Europe (1,350kt on Germany, 590kt France, 370 kt Italy, etc), while Germany dropped 74 kt of bombs including V-1 and V-2 rockets on Britain in WWII: a mere 5%, or one-twentieth as much - Dr Wesserle *The Journal of Historical Review,* 1981, vol. 2, 381-384.

<u>46 Warsaw bombing – a comparison</u>

'In fact the bombardment of Warsaw did not begin until September 26, 1939, after all the military niceties had been observed: warning leaflets dropped on to the civilian population, open routes provided for the Polish civilians to leave before the timed hour of bombardment, a formal ultimatum to the commandant of the fortress Warsaw to capitulate before the bombardment began, which was rejected'.   Irving, *Hitler's War*, 1977, 2001, 239

SELECT BIBLIO

WW1

Barnes, Harry Elmer, *The Genesis of the World War an Introduction to the Problem of War Guilt,* 1926

Steiner, Rudolf *The Karma of Untruthfulness: Secret Societies, the Media and Preparations for the Great War* December 1916 lectures, 1988,2005.

Milton, Richard *Best of Enemies Britain and Germany: 100 years of Truth and Lies* 2007

Ross, Stewart Halsey, *Propaganda for War, How the United States Was Conditioned to Fight the Great War of 1914-18*, 2009

Docherty, Gerry and MacGregor, Jim *Hidden History The Secret Origins of the First World War, 2013.*

WW2

Hoggan, David, *The Forced War*, (online) 1961,1989.

Buchanan, Patrick *Churchill, Hitler and the Unnecessary War, How Britain lost its empire and the West lost the world*, 2008.

Bradberry, Benton, *The Myth of German Villainy* 2012.

Wallendy, Uno *The Truth for Germany* (online), 2012

King, Mark , *The Bad War The truth Never Mentioned about World War 2.* 2015.

POSTSCRIPT: WILL OF THE WARMONGERS (WW2)

- <u>Harry Elmer Barnes</u> (1889-1968) *Blasting the*

Historical Blackout, 1963:

'In no country has the historical blackout been more intense and effective than in Great Britain. Here it has been ingeniously christened The Iron Curtain of Discreet Silence. Virtually nothing has been written to reveal the truth about British responsibility for the Second World War and its disastrous results.

The primary and direct responsibility for the European war, which grew into the Second World War, was almost solely that of Great Britain and the British war group, made up of both Conservatives and Labourites.

If Britain had not gratuitously given Poland a blank cheque, which was not needed in the slightest to assure British security, Poland surely might not have risked a war with Germany. Nevertheless, there would still have been no justification for British intervention in such a war or for the provocation of a European war...

The fact is that the only real offer of security which Poland received in 1938 and 1939 emanated from Hitler. He offered to guarantee the boundaries laid down in the Versailles Treaty against every other country. Even the Weimar Republic had not for a moment taken this into consideration. Whatever one may think of Hitler's government or foreign policy, no doubt exists on this point; his proposals to Poland in 1938/39 were reasonable and just and the most moderate of all which he made during the six years of his efforts to revise the Versailles Treaty by peaceful means...

- Liddell Hart (1895-1969) *History of the Second*

91

World War, 1970:

'The precise effect of the Mutual Assistance Pact was to give Poland a clear signal that aggression and belligerency was tolerable and a warning to Germany that any retaliation would be met by force...

The last thing Hitler wanted was to produce another great war. His people, and particularly his generals, were profoundly fearful of any such risk - the experiences of World War One had scarred their minds.

- David Hoggan (1923-1988) *The Forced War*, 1989:

'The secret British shift to a war policy in October 1938, when Halifax took over control of British foreign policy from Chamberlain, was followed by the public proclamation of this new policy by Chamberlain himself at Birmingham on March 17, 1939. This culminated, in turn, in the launching of the new "crusade" against Germany on September 3, 1939

Halifax in London succeeded in imposing a deliberate war policy on the British Government in 1938-1939 despite the fact that most of the leading official British experts on Germany favored a policy of Anglo-German friendship. Beck in Warsaw adopted a position of full cooperation with the war plans of Halifax despite the numerous warnings he received from Poles aghast at the prospect of witnessing their country hurtle down the road to destruction. Many efforts were made by German, French, Italian, and other European leaders to avert the catastrophe, but these efforts eventually failed, and the Halifax war policy, with the secret blessings of President Roosevelt and Marshal Stalin, emerged triumphant.

The British Government, after October 1938, repeatedly evaded acceptance of any of the commitments in the Bohemian area which had been suggested at Munich. The British Government, according to both Chamberlain and Halifax, had no right to be consulted about the Hitler-Hacha treaty of March 15, 1939, which represented, as Professor A.J.P. Taylor put it, a conservative solution of the Bohemia-Moravian problem.

The actual British foreign policy moves after March 31, 1939, were directed unrelentingly toward war. Everything possible was done to undermine several excellent opportunities for a negotiated settlement of the German-Polish dispute, and for the negotiation of a new Czech settlement based on international guarantees. Instead of working for a satisfactory agreement with Germany -- Hitler was willing to be moderate and reasonable in dealing with both the Polish and the Czech questions -- Halifax concentrated on intimidating Italy and bullying France because they both favored peace instead of war. The Polish Government was advised by Halifax to reject negotiations with Germany, and Warsaw was constantly assured that British support would be available for any war. The numerous requests of the German Government for mediation between Germany and Poland, or for a direct Anglo-German agreement, were either answered with deceptions or ignored. A maximum effort was made to present the American leaders with a distorted picture of the actual situation in Europe. All of these British moves had their roots in the obsolete, traditional policy of the balance of power.

Nevertheless, there was no time before the British

declaration of war on September 3, 1939, when Hitler would have opposed a negotiated solution with Poland. An indication of this was shown by his favorable response to the Italian conference plan on September 2, 1939, and his willingness at that time to consider an immediate armistice in Poland. His peace policy failed because the British Empire decided to challenge Germany before Hitler had completed his program of arriving at amicable understandings with his immediate neighbors

The motives of Halifax in 1939 were clearly derived from the ancient tradition of maintaining British superiority over the nations of Western and Central Europe. He had never questioned the role of his kinsman, Sir Edward Grey, in promoting World War I. Halifax did not propose to tolerate the existence in 1939 of a German Reich more prosperous and more influential than the Hohenzollern Empire which had been destroyed in 1918. It was for the prestige of Great Britain rather than for such mundane considerations as national security or immediate British interests that Halifax became a proponent of war in 1938. The traditional British aim to dominate policy in Continental Europe was the underlying reason why the world experienced the horrors of World War II.'   - p. 288 & Conclusion

- Jurgen Rieger   (1946-09) justice4germans.com, 2009

'The four-power Munich agreement, signed in September 1938: an agreement by all parties that the Sudeten Germans rightfully belonged "Heim ins Reich" (back home in the Reich.) In March 1939 both the Slovaks and the Ruthenians declared independence, whereupon the Poles invaded Czechoslovakia and occupied the Olsa Region, which was populated by Poles. The Hungarians did the same, occupying the border areas that were populated by Hungarians.

Since Czechoslovakia had ceased to exist, its President Hacha flew to Berlin on 15 March 1939 and placed the remainder of his country under the protection of the Reich. The Reich then formed the Protectorate of Bohemia and Maeren, which provided for exclusive Czech administration in all areas except military and foreign policy.

Chamberlain condemned the "German invasion" [entry of German troops in Prague on 15 March 1939] in his Birmingham speech of 17 March 1939; and on 31 March 1939 he signed an agreement with the Polish government in which Great Britain promised to support Poland in the event of war.

It is irrelevant whether Poles or Germans attacked the Gleiwitz transmitting station (whoever reads the White Book of the German-Polish war will find countless undisputed murders and assaults committed by the Poles in the weeks and months preceding 1 September 1939)

"Poland wants war with Germany and Germany will not be able to avoid it, even if it wants to." - Rydz-Smigly, Chief inspector of the Polish army in a public speech in front of Polish officers (In June 1939,)

The fact that Chamberlain, knowing of the Polish, French and American desire for war, gave a free hand to Polish war policies and did not urge Poland to accept the moderate

German demands can be explained only by the fact that he also wanted war on 1 September 1939.

Another indication of this is the fact that in Britain the evening edition of the newspaper DAILY MAIL for 31 August 1939 was confiscated. The edition had carried the story of Germany's proposals concerning the Polish Corridor as well as Poland's response, which was general mobilization. The newspaper was compelled to publish a different evening edition.[27]

Following 15 March 1939, Roosevelt exerted strong pressure on the British government to "finally exert opposition" against "Nazi tyranny" or else he would apply methods of coercion against Great Britain. It is impossible to determine precisely what threats he made, since their correspondence is still off-limits to historians (Note: According to the usually very well informed Washington journalists Drew Pearson and Robert S. Allen "the President warned that Britain could expect no more support, moral or material through the sale of airplanes, if the Munich policy continued.")

September 1, 1939: Mussolini proposes a suspension of hostilities and the immediate convening of a Conference of the Big Powers, Poland included, to discuss terms for a peaceful settlement. Germany, France and Poland immediately accept Mussolini's proposals. Britain categorically rejects any negotiations and demands withdrawal of German troops from all occupied Polish territory (30 kilometers deep). Note: Britain does not consult

---

[27] I have not been able to verify this, NK

with Warsaw before making its decision.'

- <u>Steve F.,</u> Background to the Munich Agreement:

'The dismemberment of Germany following the Great War meant that the Sudetenland (Bohemia and Moravia), part of Germany for 700 years and with a population of over 3 million Germans, were moved -- against their wishes -- out of their homeland to become part of a newly-created country, populated mainly by Czechs and Slovaks, which was to be called Czecho-Slovakia.

The Sudeten Germans suffered greatly under Czech rule. On March 4th, 1919, public meetings calling for self determination were brutally broken up and 52 German civilians were murdered. Lord Rothermere described Czechoslovakia as a 'swindle.'

Conditions imposed upon the Sudeten-Germans were so harsh that during 1919, 600,000 were forced to leave their settlements of centuries. Throughout the ensuing years, the Czech President, M. Benes, saw to it that conditions became so intolerable that even England and France felt it necessary to concede this injustice of Versailles and agreed to its return to Germany.

"The worst offence was the subjection of over three million Germans to Czech rule." -- H.N Brailsford, Leading left wing commentator

The Czech administration which wanted the German territory but not its population, agreed, but refused to do so and

97

instead began a reign of terror aimed at driving the German population over the borders into Hitler's Germany in a program that has since been termed ethnic cleansing.

When under the terms of the Versailles Treaty, a large part of Germany and its German population was awarded to Poland, so began an anti-German racist pogrom resulting in widespread murder and mayhem resulting in over a million Germans being 'ethnically cleansed' from their homelands of centuries.

Hitler's Germany could no longer act as bystanders to the grim unfolding tragedy. When German troops re-entered their former territory, the Sudetenland, there was rejoicing in the streets.' - CODOH page 'Hitler's Peace offers vs Unconditional surrender', April 2016, in the WW2 section, quoted with kind permission.

- <u>Udo Walendy</u> (1927 -) *Who Started World War Two? truth for a war-torn world,* 2014. Permission to quote kindly given by Castle Hill Press.

'Poland was not going to wait for the outcome of the Versailles Peace conference that was stretching over many months and, instead, used the armistice of Germany to occupy the Posen region and parts of western Prussia ... The Versailles Peace conference accepted from Poland the fait accompli, with the stipulation, however, that the transfer of territory was made dependent on the Polish obligation of having to guarantee to the German and Jewish minorities far-reaching independence and the preservation of their national culture and traditional way of life' (p.134) Clearly that did not happen so even under the terms of the Versailles Treaty the Polish occupation of that land was unlawful.

At Versailles, the British Prime Minister Lloyd George had remarked: "I tell you once more, we would never have thought of giving to Poland a province that had not been Polish for the last 900 years... The proposal of the Polish Commission that we should place 2,100,000 Germans under the control of a people which is of a different religion and which has never proved its capacity for stable self-government throughout its history, must, in my judgment, lead sooner or later to a new war in the East of Europe..." Compare this with Woodrow Wilson's words of 7 April 1919: "France's only real interest in Poland was to weaken Germany by giving the Poles areas to which they had no claim." The U.S. Secretary of State, Robert Lansing, remarked on 8 May 1919: "Do examine the treaty and you will find that whole populations, against their will, were delivered into the power of those who hated them, while their economic resources were snatched away and handed over to others.' - p.134-6

NK: This unfair Versailles treaty was not the cause of a world war. It was the cause only of a local conflict between Poland and Germany - It was the British will, that transformed a local European conflict, here deemed by Lloyd George to have been inevitable, into a world war – or, such has here been my argument.

18459388R00058

Printed in Great Britain
by Amazon